TOXIC

to

Transformed

100 WORDS OF LIFE TO RENEW THE MIND

A Verbal and Emotional Abuse Recovery Devotional

Donna L Lewis

BIBLICAL CITATIONS

JOIN OUR MAILING LIST

We have exciting things on the horizon! Stay in the loop and join our mailing list! As a token of my gratitude you will receive a very special gift as well as FREE offers and special advance pricing on new books and devotionals.

www.toxictotransformedlife.com

DEDICATION

This work of love is dedicated to those overcoming the toxic aftermath of verbal and emotional abuse.

You have withstood the heat and not given in!

May you be blessed abundantly beyond all you can ask, hope, think, or imagine. With all my heart,

Donna L Lewis

TABLE OF CONTENTS

INTRODUCTION

In my experience, few things rival the damage of verbal and emotional abuse. It acts like a wrecking ball, demolishing identity, blowing out confidence, and shattering self-worth. The ones fortunate enough to escape are left in ruins, wondering if the pieces will ever fit back together.

Toxic programming cages the mind with false belief systems. As a result, survivors are often plagued by anxiety, never knowing when their calm will be stolen. Shame and false guilt blockade life-giving relationships. And possibly worst of all, dreams are discarded along with the God-given potential inside. In order to be set free, a survivor requires total transformation!

The apostle Paul teaches in 2 Corinthians 1:3–4 that we comfort others with the same comfort God has given us. Raised in a home where verbal battery ran amuck, followed by over ten years in an emotionally abusive marriage, I know the devastation and have lived inside the cage. But more importantly, I know the freedom of transformation.

I am a living example of the renewing power of God's Word. I have gone from fearful to fearless, hopeless to hopeful, and unloved to much loved! That, my friend, is only the tip of the iceberg! I have learned to dream again and have watched in wonder as God began to bring fulfillment!

Dare to dream! Dare to imagine living the life Christ Jesus promised in John 10:10. He said, *"A thief has only one thing in mind—he wants to steal, slaughter, and destroy. But I have come to give you everything in abundance, more than you expect—life in its fullness until you overflow!"* Are you ready to live? *Really* live, until life is splashing all around you with the overflow.

I am here to declare, not only is it possible, it's a God-given guarantee! The Word of God is a miraculous, living thing with the power of metamorphosis. It is here for you today!

This devotional serves as a catalyst. Working through each page, you will learn to hear the voice of your Creator. As you listen to His voice, a whole new world will open as the revelation of your true identity comes into view! You are an adored child of God, crowned with authority. You have purpose! You are important! You are a royal citizen of the Kingdom of God!

Confidence will multiply as you learn God has fully equipped you for every task. You will begin to understand God's plan for boundaries, discernment, even managing panic attacks.

Most exciting of all, you will believe God loves your dreams! You will see that He placed them in your heart for "such a time as this."

It all begins with renewing the mind. Why live one more day caged in the toxic aftermath of verbal and emotional abuse? Transformation provides wings to freedom. It's time to fly!

THIS DEVOTIONAL

Devotionals are catalysts intended to stimulate deeper thinking and awareness. They guide and inspire; they do not draw conclusions or ask you to engage in deep analysis. This devotional is not written as an exposition on the subject of verbal and emotional abuse. It is a starting point of healing and transformation.

Transformation happens as you, the reader, draw into the presence of Christ, allowing the Holy Spirit to apply and personalize these truths. The direction and conclusion will be entirely unique to you because it's a custom fit!

There are 100 "Words of Life" with guided journal entries and exercises. These are intended to facilitate a deeper awareness of the truths contained in each page.

You are in charge! You know what is going to facilitate transformation and healing best for you. If you want to speed through the devotional in one sitting and then go back to digest each word, go for it! If you want to chew for days on one page and then slowly move to the next, that's perfect!

Bottom line: work through this devotional at your pace, your way! You can complete the journal entries in written form, or if you're more artistic and visual, do a drawing or water color exploring the questions.

Periodically, I will ask you to share your entries with me. Only do this if you feel comfortable and want to. If you decide you would like to share, just go to *toxictotransformedlife.com*!

Here are two frequently used terms within this devotional.

GOD'S WORD:

His spoken Word planted within you through the Holy Spirit. God speaks to you daily through His living Word, that "still small voice," and through His written Word, the Holy Bible. Both are huge in transforming your mind!

WORD OF LIFE:

This is another name for God's Word, but for the purpose of this devotional, it used as a description. Words of life are the kind of words you want flowing into your life and out of your mouth. They give and do not take away. They are full of encouragement, love, kindness, and helpful instruction. They build and do not tear down. They always leave the listener better for having heard them!

THE WAY OF CHRIST

Christ is the way of transformation. This devotional will make absolutely NO sense without Him! The Holy Spirit that flows from Him is essential in this process, allowing you to comprehend the Word of God. If you have not already come to understand Jesus—the Anointed One, God's only Son—as your personal Lord and savior, allow me to introduce you to Him.

He was born as a physical baby, the Word of God in human form. He died on the cross so that He could kill the power of unloving deeds, also known as sin. He rose from the dead, opening the doorway for access to eternal life so we may be spiritually reborn a son or daughter of God!

In order to receive the precious gift of personal relationship with Him and receive the power of the Holy Spirit, you must do the following:

THE STEPS OF NEW LIFE IN CHRIST

1. Acknowledge that you have fallen short of perfect loving deeds. This is sin.

2. Ask God to forgive you through the sacrifice of Jesus on the cross.

3. Confess Jesus Christ as your Lord and savior and believe from the heart that He is raised physically from the dead.

4. Ask to be filled by God's powerful Holy Spirit and invite Him to renew and transform your mind and heart.

Pray with me:

"Dear Jesus, I know I have fallen short in following Your law of love. I have sinned against myself and others and therefore against You. I confess I am heartbroken over my failure to follow Your ways. I understand I am powerless to do what pleases You on my own. I know in my humanness I need more power than I possess. I need a new heart and a new mind. I know You desire to give me these. I believe that You are God's son and that You died on the cross to take the justice for my sins. I know and believe You rose again, making a way for me to be transformed. I ask to be forgiven of my sins and forever changed into a son/daughter of God, just like You. I want to live forever with You, Jesus, just like You promised. Please fill me now with Your Holy Spirit. Empower me to understand and follow Your Words of Life. Thank You! In Your Name, Jesus, Amen."

If you have prayed this prayer, please contact me! I want to make sure you have everything you need to prosper in your new life with Jesus Christ!

Read the Gospel of John and the book of Romans (both found in the New Testament); these further elaborate on the steps you just made. This devotional will also explain much of the miracle that just happened in your life!

Blessings abundant to you, my friend! I love you! I am praying that these words of life will heal and restore your mind and take you on a marvelous, empowering journey from *Toxic to Transformed!*

One

YOUR STORY IS NOT FINISHED

We stood before a breathtaking, high desert waterfall. My friend, Amanda and I made an impromptu escape from Portland, taking refuge at the Deschutes River.

Gazing into the rapids, cool sprays of whitewater tickled my cheek. I wondered out loud, "Do you think this is what God does with our tears?" Amanda looked at me quizzically, "What do you mean?" "Does He turn them into waterfalls, like this; something beautiful?"

The past year had left me crying torrents. My identity to that point had been defined by the toxins of verbal and emotional abuse. I was raised in a verbally and emotionally abusive home, then spent 10 years in an emotionally abusive marriage which ended in divorce. My world was in ruins. Tears were main course meals. I needed hope.

I am thinking, you can relate. Does it feel like your tears could fill a river, or maybe an ocean?

Watching cool mountain water gushing over rocks and boulders, I could see God doing the same with my heart. He desired to flow over it with never-ending streams of love, truth and acceptance. In that moment, I believed He would transform my sorrow into a healing balm.

Our Heavenly Father, in His immutable word, makes this promise to us over and over again: Restoration, healing and transformation.

My story was not finished, and your story is not finished either, indeed, the best parts begin today!

"Fear not; you will no longer live in shame. Don't be afraid; there is no more disgrace for you. You will no longer remember the shame of your youth and the sorrows of widowhood. For your Creator will be your husband; the Lord of Heaven's Armies is his name! He is your Redeemer, the Holy One of Israel, the God of all the earth. For the Lord has called you back from your grief."
—Isaiah 54:4–6, NLT

JOURNAL: List three goals you would like to accomplish through this devotional.

Two

ROYALTY

Being reborn through Christ Jesus means we are eternally changed. The shame and guilt are washed away in a tidal wave of God's amazing grace. Jesus took all of it on the cross, and it died with Him there. When Jesus resurrected, He opened a supernatural doorway of eternal life for you and me! Spectacular!

In that awesome moment, a completely new reality is born. A whole new state of being! You are now a son or daughter of the most-high God. You are His prize possession, a precious jewel beautifying His crown. You are accepted and walk in His favor. You are royalty. You have been entrusted with authority. You have vital purpose!

"But you are God's chosen treasure—priests who are kings, a spiritual "nation" set apart as God's devoted ones. He called you out of darkness to experience his marvelous light, and now he claims you as his very own. He did this so that you would broadcast his glorious wonders throughout the world."
—1 Peter 2:9, TPT

JOURNAL: When you think of yourself as royalty, what comes to mind?

Three

IT'S A NEW DAY

It's a new day! There is so much to look forward to! Truly, the best days are ahead as you immerse yourself in God's Word. These precious words of life are infused with powerful grace and truth.

The Holy Spirit smears them like healing salve upon your mind, soul, and spirit. His power transforms you into a person of destiny, authority, and purpose!

"For I know the thoughts and plans that I have for you, says the Lord, thoughts and plans for welfare and peace and not for evil, to give you hope in your final outcome."
—Jeremiah 29:11, AMPC

JOURNAL: Write down what comes to mind as you meditate on these three words:

Destiny

Authority

Purpose

How do you see yourself as a person of destiny, authority, and purpose?

VALLEY OF THE SHADOW OF DEATH

The journey from toxic to transformed passes through the "Valley of the Shadow of Death." As you trudge through trauma, it could feel very threatening. You may be tempted to quit half way, but don't give up. The way to healing and renewal is through the valley, all the way, to the other side.

Remember, you are never alone. The Good Shepherd is leading and will not abandon you. Stay close and do not bolt off in fear. Trust Him! He is guiding you into a prosperous, wonderful life!

> *"Lord, even when your path takes me through the valley of deepest darkness, fear will never conquer me, for you already have! You remain close to me and lead me through it all the way. Your authority is my strength and my peace. The comfort of your love takes away my fear. I'll never be lonely, for you are near."*
> *—Psalm 23:4, TPT*

JOURNAL: The road to recovery can feel at times like walking through the Valley of the Shadow of Death. What have been three of the darkest moments for you along this road?

Jesus, the Good Shepherd, promises to lead you through the deepest darkness. Name three ways He has shown Himself faithful to you on the journey from toxic to transformed.

Five

BECOME AN EXPERT

You become an expert at your own recovery as you do the homework, dive into research, and receive counsel!

Being surrounded by wise consultants creates confidence. Especially as you walk through healing and transformation. They will expose potential obstacles and hidden dangers. They will validate your experience and provide clarity in times of confusion.

Solomon, Israel's wisest king, stated, "In the abundance of counselors there is safety." Collective wisdom opens your eyes, enabling you to move forward decisively with purpose!

> *"Without consultation, plans are frustrated, but with many counselors they succeed."*
> *—Proverbs 15:22, NASB*

JOURNAL: List five resources you are currently using as "wise counselors" in your recovery. These may include a mentor, a recovery group, or even virtual resources like YouTube channels, Facebook pages, authors, or bloggers.

Please feel free to share with me at *toxictotransformedlife.com*! The more resources, the better!

Six

GOD'S WORD IS MEDICINE

God's Word is the single best asset for renewing your thought life and countering any lies you may have come to believe. The Holy Spirit opens your mind so that you may fully embrace the life-giving knowledge of Christ!

Think of it this way: All the toxic messaging internalized over the years is poison. God's Word is medicine, slowly but surely cleansing your system and transforming the cells of your mind. Once sick and dying, now they are beautiful and fully alive!

> *"Once your life was full of sin's darkness, but now you have the very light of our Lord shining through you because of your union with him. Your mission is to live as children flooded with his revelation-light! And the supernatural fruits of his light will be seen in you—goodness, righteousness, and truth. Then you will learn to choose what is beautiful to our Lord."*
> *—Ephesians 5:8–10, TPT, emphasis added*

JOURNAL: Memorizing scripture is wholly transformative. Run an internet search, "Bible verses for the mind." Write down three you will commit to memory.

If memorization is new to you, I recommend picking short ones that flow in an easy rhythm. The book of Proverbs is loaded with great options!

Seven

TRANSFORMING THE MIND

Transforming the mind means rejecting the false and replacing it with truth. You learn to recognize deceptive reasoning and other thought patterns that inspire destructive behavior. Destructive behavior can also be defined as sin because it falls short of God's highest ideal, which is love.

God desires you to walk in perfect love. In perfect love you are kind to yourself and others. You think as He thinks and behave as He behaves. You are a perfect reflection of His nature.

As this new life-giving information bonds to your thought life, you see transformation. You don't think the same, act the same, or even look the same. You are new!

> *"Those who are dominated by the sinful nature think about sinful things,*
> *but those who are controlled by the Holy Spirit think about things that please*
> *the Spirit. So letting your sinful nature control your mind leads to death.*
> *But letting the Spirit control your mind leads to life and peace."*
> *—Romans 8:5–6, NLT*

JOURNAL: List three thought patterns you desire to overcome.

Now, run an internet search for three relevant scriptures addressing those patterns. For example, you might search "Bible verses on fear."

List the scripture references with a short paraphrase of each verse.

Eight

LIFE WITHOUT LIMITS

The desire of Christ is for you to live with purpose and freedom. As you meditate and internalize the Word of God, you are being transformed into His likeness. The likeness of God, with whom, "all things are possible"! (Matthew 19:26)

Think of it! The Word of God removes all the toxic restraints, liberating you to become the full expression of His grace and truth on planet Earth. This new, transformed state of being is a life without limits!

> ***"You are being renewed in the spirit of your minds; you put on the new self,***
> ***the one created according to God's likeness in righteousness and purity of the truth."***
> ***—Ephesians 4:23–24, HCSB***

JOURNAL: What are some personal limitations you have come to believe about yourself?

How are you liberated from those limits as you "put on the new self" according to Ephesians 4:24?

Nine

FREEDOM FROM CONFUSION

You have within yourself something extraordinary: the very Spirit of God! That Spirit has a specific purpose. The Holy Spirit is given to provide counsel, comfort, instruction, and great power!

You never need to be confused. You have direct, unhindered access to the heart and mind of God! Imagine! God, who possesses all wisdom, understanding, and knowledge! Every answer is found in Him; just ask and wait patiently. Be confident, the answer will come!

> *"No one can know a person's thoughts except that person's own spirit, and no one can know God's thoughts except God's own Spirit. And we have received God's Spirit (not the world's spirit), so we can know the wonderful things God has freely given us."*
> *—1 Corinthians 2:11–12, NLT*

JOURNAL: List three things you feel when you're confused. It may be a sense of emotional distress or a physical feeling like a racing heart or pounding head.

What fears are associated with those feelings?

Run an Internet search for "Bible verses when I'm afraid." Write one of them below.

Ten

AN EVICTION NOTICE TO ANXIETY

God almighty, in perfect love, fills you by His Spirit. Anxiety has no home in the presence of perfect love! As you follow the liberating principles of God's love, fear loses governing power!

Cruel deception is replaced by the kindness of truth. Confident faith replaces self-destructive doubt. Life-giving hope replaces worry. You are complete and lack nothing in the purity of God's love.

"By your mighty power I can walk through any devastation and you will keep me alive, reviving me. Your power set me free from the hatred of my enemies. You keep every promise you've ever made to me! Since your love for me is constant and endless, I ask you, Lord, to finish every good thing that you've begun in me!"
—Psalm 138:7–8, TPT

JOURNAL: Describe a way God has demonstrated to you personally His overwhelming love.

Eleven

REMEMBER TRIUMPH

Memory: the capacity to call to mind wonderous events in the theater of your mind! Take ground from the enemy as you remember every triumph of the Lord. Gain victory as you replay His sweet consolations. Build faith as you meditate on the limitless power of our God. Remember triumph!

"So I say to my soul, 'Don't be discouraged. Don't be disturbed. For I know my God will break through for me.' Then I'll have plenty of reasons to praise him all over again. Yes, living before his face is my saving grace!"
—Psalm 42:11, TPT

JOURNAL: List as many victories from the Lord as you can in 2 minutes. Set a timer and go!

Twelve

THE POWER OF ENDURANCE

It takes endurance to win a race or complete a degree. Renewing the mind is no different; it too requires patient endurance. The world will challenge your resolve as you walk through the process of transformation. It will try to reinforce old lies and double down on self-doubt, — but your confidence lies in a power greater than your own. Look to the One who has overcome the world: Jesus Christ! Focus your attention on Him and His eternal supply; then you too will overcome!

> *"You need the strength of endurance to reveal the poetry of God's will and then you receive the promise in full."*
> *—Hebrews 10:36, TPT*

JOURNAL: Run an Internet search for "promises of God from the Bible." Write down five of these promises and select one to memorize.

NEW LIFE, NEW ALLIES

The old is dead and gone forever, along with toxic shame and guilt. This new life is so beautiful! So glorious!

It is a life of pure love, pure power, and pure strength of mind. It is a life full of faith in all God is capable and willing to do on your behalf!

It is a life where the entire force of heaven is rooting for you, empowering you, and equipping you as you fulfill your calling. You cannot lose!

"And now, just as you accepted Christ Jesus as your Lord, you must continue to follow him. Let your roots grow down into him, and let your lives be built on him. Then your faith will grow strong in the truth you were taught, and you will overflow with thankfulness."
—Colossians 2:6–7, NLT

JOURNAL: In what specific area of your life can you apply God's love, power and strength?

For example: *"I will apply God's pure love to experience His complete acceptance so that my wounds of rejection will heal."* Feel free to list related scripture as well.

Fourteen

FULLY EQUIPPED

You have every tool at your disposal; you lack nothing! You are fully equipped to accomplish the God-given purpose of your life. You must not allow voices of the past to silence you with intimidation or deceive you into believing you are not adequate!

The truth is, God supplies everything amply, in full, through Christ! Because His Spirit dwells happily within you, you are more than enough!

> *"Yet we don't see ourselves as capable enough to do anything in our own strength, for our true competence flows from God's empowering presence. He alone makes us adequate ministers who are focused on an entirely new covenant. Our ministry is not based on the letter of the law but through the power of the Spirit. The letter of the law kills, but the Spirit pours out life."*
> *—2 Corinthians 3:5–6, TPT*

JOURNAL: Consider the difference between self-reliance and God-reliance. How does the invitation to rely on the competence of God inspire and empower you?

REMAIN IN THE VINE

There are no limits to what you can accomplish through the Kingdom-power of Jesus Christ! With God all things are possible! There is nothing but hope because you are joined to God through Christ Jesus.

God listens with intent interest when you speak to Him. He is deeply concerned with everything that concerns you. He delights in the same things that delight you! My friend let's agree to stay close and stay connected to the nourishing, powerful love of Jesus!

> *"I am the sprouting vine and you're my branches. As you live in union with me as your source, fruitfulness will stream from within you— but when you live separated from me you are powerless."*
> *—John 15:5, TPT*

JOURNAL: Describe how you see yourself living in union with Christ Jesus. When you imagine yourself as a branch sprouting from Jesus as a vine, what does that picture inspire within you?

Sixteen

IN LOVE WITH TRUTH

Jesus is truth; therefore, as His disciple, your deepest longing must be truth! Because of the Holy Spirit, you fundamentally know when something is off. The key is to trust that intuition and investigate! Does what you are hearing or reading line up with God's Word, God's nature, God's values?

Truth is fresh, clean, and unencumbered. It flows freely and restores the listener. Though it may be difficult or even painful to encounter truth, the relief of freedom from bondage soon follows. Truth is life! And like an ever-flowing, crystal-clean river, the more you drink, the more you receive!

"Then on the most important day of the feast, the last day, Jesus stood and shouted out to the crowds—'All you thirsty ones, come to me! Come to me and drink! Believe in me so that rivers of living water will burst out from within you, flowing from your innermost being, just like the Scripture says!"
—John 7:37–38, TPT

JOURNAL: Describe how you feel when you hear truth and it fully connects with you. How do you feel physically? What goes through your mind?

Seventeen

THE MIND OF TRUTH

Truth is inflexible. This can be a troubling reality when you want to bend the truth—squish it just a little—to fit your needs. In order to be set free, you must be willing to open your mind and accept revelatory knowledge from God's Word. You must conform your mind to fit the truth. In so doing, there is liberty, beautiful and sweet!

"Jesus said to those Jews who believed in him, 'When you continue to embrace all that I teach, you prove that you are my true followers. For if you embrace the truth, it will release more freedom into your lives."
—John 8:31–32, TPT

JOURNAL: When have you squished the truth to fit your needs? List practical ways you will conform your mind to truth from now on.

Eighteen

PERFECTLY PREPARED

God has big plans for your life, but before you begin, there must be training and outfitting. He is love and therefore will never send you unprepared. The Word of God is a training manual, tool kit, nutrition, and first aid—everything you need for every situation! You are perfectly prepared to become a leading light when you familiarize yourself with this marvelous resource!

"Every Scripture has been inspired by the Holy Spirit, the breath of God. It will empower you by its instruction and correction, giving you the strength to take the right direction and lead you deeper into the path of godliness. Then you will be God's servant, fully mature and perfectly prepared to fulfill any assignment God gives you."
—2 Timothy 3:16–17, TPT

JOURNAL: Describe how God's Word is supplying each of the following in your life:

Training

Tools

Nutrition

First Aid

Nineteen

ICE CREAM!

To know God, you must know His Word and be filled by His Spirit. Together, God's Word and Spirit unveil the truth of His essence: who He is and what He values.

Learn the way He operates, even how it feels when He enters a room! Recognize His voice and fall in love with His instruction. Long for His Word and crave it as you would your favorite ice cream sundae!

> *"The rarest treasures of life are found in his truth. That's why I prize God's word like others prize the finest gold. Nothing brings the soul such sweetness as seeking his living words."*
> *—Psalm 19:10, TPT*

EXERCISE: What's your favorite ice cream treat? If you don't like ice cream, that's okay; just list a favorite sweet!

When you think about that special treat, what feelings does it inspire? Can you taste it in your mouth? Smell it? Do you feel a tiny little burst of excitement run through you? Maybe you're even getting hungry! Mmmm……..!!! Describe it!

Now, using that tasty example, how does God's Word and presence nourish your mind and please your soul?

Twenty
MEASURELESS GRACE

The arms of God embrace galaxies, yet the tiniest animal does not go unnoticed! With eyes of pure compassion, He sees each one and meets their need.

When He looks at you, one created in His image, His love is far greater! If your mind is troubled, He longs to provide peace. Measureless grace is available to you today and every day!

> *"Look at all the birds—do you think they worry about their existence?*
> *They don't plant or reap or store up food, yet your heavenly Father provides them*
> *each with food. Aren't you much more valuable to your Father than they?"*
> *—Matthew 6:26, TPT*

EXERCISE: What is troubling you today? Remember, it can be little or small; size does not matter—it's all the same to God!

In the space below, send Him a quick text describing the struggle, just as you would to a close friend. God is interested and ready to supply all you need!

Twenty-One

THE WOLF SLAYER

Old memories of rejection and humiliation charge the mind like snarling wolves. The anxiety overwhelms; with head pounding, you long to hide somewhere you'll never be found. Beloved, I've found the perfect place!

The Word of God tells us, *"The name of the Lord is a strong tower, the righteous runs into it and is safe!"* (Proverbs 18:10, NASB, emphasis added).

Christ is the wolf slayer, your mighty warrior, your strong defense. As you run to Him, these dark beasts vanish into His eternal light!

"You're as real to me as bedrock beneath my feet, like a castle on a cliff, my forever firm fortress, my mountain of hiding, my pathway of escape, my tower of rescue where none can reach me. My secret strength and shield around me, you are salvation's ray of brightness shining on the hillside, always the champion of my cause. All I need to do is to call to you, singing to you, the praiseworthy God. When I do, I'm safe and sound in you."
—Psalms 18:2–3, TPT

JOURNAL: Are any vicious memories or thoughts chasing you?

Take them now to the throne of God and visualize yourself laying them at His feet. List them.

Now, listen as the Lord speaks over them. Jesus cursed a fig tree that did not bear fruit (Mark 11:12–25); these thoughts and memories are a fruitless fig tree!

What is the Lord saying to you? Write it down and then read it out loud.

INDEPENDENCE DAY

What is pinning you down? Is there a condition or situation holding you like a snare with tight, burning ropes? A relationship? An addiction? Poisonous thought patterns? I have good news: Today is your personal 4th of July! It is Independence Day, my love!

Now is the time! Cut the ropes! Declare your emancipation with one thunderous holler and take to the wind!

It's time to soar with falcons and scream with eagles! You have all the tools. You have the power to do this. You have the sword of God's Word. You have the Spirit of Liberty, who is the Holy Spirit. Freedom begins today!

"So we must let go of every wound that has pierced us and the sin we so easily fall into. Then we will be able to run life's marathon race with passion and determination, for the path has been already marked out before us."
—Hebrews 12:1, TPT

JOURNAL: Write your personal Declaration of Independence.

Read it out loud, sign and date it.

Celebrate your freedom! Do a dance, lift up a shout, light off fire-crackers!

Do something to memorialize and celebrate this momentous day. Tell me about it! Go to *toxictotransformedlife.com*.

RUN WILD!

Let dreams run wild! Our Heavenly Papa delights in dreams! Share them freely. Don't hold back. Prattle on endlessly, describe every detail, leave nothing out!

God will never grow bored or give a dull, blank stare. He will not shoot your dreams down, describing all the ways they could fail. No, He is eternally interested and invested! He can't wait to encourage all your ideas and, even more, empower them to come alive!

"Never doubt God's mighty power to work in you and accomplish all this. He will achieve infinitely more than your greatest request, your most unbelievable dream, and exceed your wildest imagination. He will outdo them all, for his miraculous power constantly energizes you."
—Ephesians 3:20, TPT

JOURNAL: What are your dreams? Quickly, without second guessing and no editing—that's cheating! — list the first three that come to mind.

Twenty-Four

FRESH SPRING

You inspire! You are an influence! You bring a shift into each room you walk into! You carry love, compassion, and wisdom from God within the temple of your body! Allow His presence to flow through you in faith. Move as a unified team with His Spirit. The fresh spring resulting from this supernatural union will enhance and beautify everyone it touches!

"Discover creative ways to encourage others and to motivate them toward
acts of compassion, doing beautiful works as expressions of love."
—Hebrews 10:24, TPT

JOURNAL: What are some ways you are uniquely equipped to inspire others? Don't allow self-doubt or dismissive thoughts to contain your imagination. Just write down what comes to mind.

Twenty-Five

CHOSEN

You are chosen—hand-picked by God the Father! You are not forgotten, left behind, or left out. You are His prize! His favorite gift! His very own!

"I knew you before I formed you in your mother's womb. Before you were born I set you apart and appointed you as my prophet to the nations."
—Jeremiah 1:5, NLT, emphasis added

EXERCISE: Read this verse again, replacing "you" with your name.

Describe the emotions and thoughts it evokes.

Twenty-Six

VITAL PURPOSE

Leadership is about influencing others in the same way that Christ influences you. Your Creator had a high function in mind when He fashioned you! It is unique to you and will flow naturally from the vessel He created you to be!

You do not have to force it or be in fear that it won't work. You can have abundant confidence in your manufacturer. He does everything with the highest attention to excellence. All you have to do is stay connected to Him and let His power flow!

"You are the body of the Anointed One, and each of you is a unique and vital part of it."
—1 Corinthians 12:27, TPT

JOURNAL: How have you experienced the influence of Christ?

How will you continue to cultivate His influence in your life?

Twenty-Seven

DISTRACTION OR FULFILLMENT?

I have heard it said, and find it to be true, that not every opportunity is a God opportunity. You must listen to the Holy Spirit and ask, "is this a distraction from or a fulfillment of your purpose?"

"If you need wisdom, ask our generous God, and he will give it to you. He will not rebuke you for asking. But when you ask him, be sure that your faith is in God alone. Do not waver, for a person with divided loyalty is as unsettled as a wave of the sea that is blown and tossed by the wind."
—James 1:5–6, NLT

JOURNAL: What practical steps are you taking to ensure you say yes to God opportunities and no to distractions?

Twenty-Eight

FREE FROM THE MAZE

Have you ever felt stuck, trapped in a maze, with every turn another dead end? This is the time to access the Holy Spirit and inquire of God! Seek Him with tenacious patience and be willing to wait. The answer will come, as sure as there is a morning!

> *"I hear the Lord saying, 'I will stay close to you, instructing and guiding you along the pathway for your life. I will advise you along the way and lead you forth with my eyes as your guide. So don't make it difficult; don't be stubborn when I take you where you've not been before. Don't make me tug you and pull you along. Just come with me!"*
> *—Psalm 32:8–9, TPT*

JOURNAL: Describe a previous maze-like experience.

What feeling did it produce?

What thoughts went through your mind?

As you meditate on Psalm 32:8–9, how do you visualize God working in your situation today?

Twenty-Nine

DECLARING PEACE

The battle is real. Like Jekyll and Hyde, you are fully capable of being your own worst enemy! Self-condemnation, conflicting emotions, and anger all attempt to sabotage God's best for your life. You must establish terms of peace within yourself. Through careful, pin-point application of God's Word, you can end the carnage and walk in the abundant life Christ promises!

> *"For we have the living Word of God, which is full of energy, and it pierces more sharply than a two-edged sword. It will even penetrate to the very core of our being where soul and spirit, bone and marrow meet! It interprets and reveals the true thoughts and secret motives of our hearts."*
> *—Hebrews 4:12, TPT*

JOURNAL: What actions and attitudes are preventing you from enjoying peace and abundant life?

List three scriptures that can help you refocus on the true identity you have in Christ.

Thirty

TRUSTED FRIEND

The Word of God is your best friend, greatest teacher, and most trusted counselor. Through the Word of God, your mind is healed and renewed! God's Word weaves the threads of your life together into a dazzling tapestry—a masterpiece!

Ugly gashes of cruelty are healed by an encounter with God's loving kindness. Distortions fade into the clarity of truth! Your response to situations shifts from fear to faith, doubt to confidence, panic to peace! As you internalize God's Word, speak it, and write it down, everything changes! There is nothing more powerful!

"Every Scripture has been written by the Holy Spirit, the breath of God. It will empower you by its instruction and correction, giving you the strength to take the right direction and lead you deeper into the path of godliness. Then you will be God's servant, fully mature and perfectly prepared to fulfill any assignment God gives you."
—2 Timothy 3:16–17, TPT

JOURNAL: Think carefully; are there any behaviors connected to toxic belief systems that need to be transformed in your life?

Write them down with a corresponding scripture that you will commit to memory.

Thirty-One
LADY WISDOM

Lady Wisdom is a fierce and trusted defender. She will never fail to protect you from seductive deception. You can build a relationship with her through consistent interaction.

You will find her in the company of mentors, teachers, and friends who have a proven track record of integrity and knowledge. Nurture her through prayer and application of God's Word.

Wisdom requires patient attention, but if you treat her with care, she will keep you alive!

"If you do what I say you will live well. Guard your life with my revelation-truth, for my teaching is as precious as your eyesight. Treasure my instructions, and cherish them within your heart. Say to wisdom, 'I love you,' and to understanding, 'You're my sweetheart. May the two of you protect me, and may we never be apart!'"
—Proverbs 7:2–5, TPT

JOURNAL: Go to the book of Proverbs in the Old Testament of the Bible. Scholars categorize this among the Wisdom books of the Bible. Scan over chapters 1–5 and write down three verses you will commit to memory.

Thirty-Two

GRACE & TRUTH

Christ is grace and truth. He cleans old wounds and liberates the mind. In Him you have freedom to explore and realize all that is good, pure, kind, and creative. As you remain transfixed in His gaze, your thoughts are filled with "life and life to the full"!

"So keep your thoughts continually fixed on all that is authentic and real, honorable and admirable, beautiful and respectful, pure and holy, merciful and kind. And fasten your thoughts on every glorious work of God, praising him always."
—Philippians 4:8, TPT

JOURNAL: What is cluttering the closet of your mind? Think about influences. What is taking up valuable space? It could be anything: a person, a television show, some other media. Choose three to box up and clear out!

Thirty-Three
ABUNDANT PRODUCTIVITY

You are filled with the Holy Spirit and therefore equipped with all power, wisdom, and knowledge to walk out the life of Christ Jesus. As you draw near with a listening ear and a responsive heart, you experience His transforming power.

Drinking in His rich words, you become more and more aware of His mind and personality. You become intuitive of His desires and quick to fulfill them! The end result is abundant productivity within His Kingdom and the most amazing sense of satisfaction and fulfillment!

> *"Since these virtues are already planted deep within, and you possess them in abundant supply, they will keep you from being inactive or fruitless in your pursuit of knowing Jesus Christ more intimately."*
> *—2 Peter 1:8, TPT*

JOURNAL: How do you spend time with Jesus? Describe a typical day.

What would make your time with Him even more meaningful? Prayerfully consider which activities would be right for you and write them down.

Here are a few creative ideas many find effective as they draw near to Christ:

Speaking words of praise and worship, singing, worshipful dancing, prayerful listening, journaling, memorizing scripture, creating devotional art, soaking in worship music and recorded scripture, writing poetry and music.

THE BODY OF CHRIST

You and I and all other believers join together to make up the body of Christ Jesus, who is absolute truth and love. Surrender your life to His nature, giving Him complete authority over your motives, thoughts, and emotions. As you do, your community and you as an individual will experience glorious transformation! Your capacity for empathy expands, your compassion deepens, and your patience is maximized. You are not the same!

"You are always and dearly loved by God! So robe yourself with virtues of God, since you have been divinely chosen to be holy. Be merciful as you endeavor to understand others, and be compassionate, showing kindness toward all. Be gentle and humble, unoffendable in your patience with others."
—Colossians 3:12, TPT, emphasis added

JOURNAL: What are three areas of your life that you need to surrender to God? Look at the scripture above for inspiration.

A MAGNIFICENT FEAST

The moment you step into relationship with Christ Jesus, His life and His word begin a miraculous work. First, you are reborn into something completely new. Your heart is softened to receive pure, sweet love and truth.

Then, as you feast on the Word of God, the Holy Spirit takes that nutritious food and begins transforming your thoughts from death to life, from hopeless to hopeful! Your whole perspective shifts, and you discover that all things are possible!

"Do not be conformed to this world but be transformed by the renewing of your mind, so that you may discern what is the will of God—what is good and acceptable and perfect."
—Romans 12:2, TLV

JOURNAL: Describe your feast and transformation process so far.

Where have you experienced the greatest renewal?

Thirty-Six

YOU BELONG

My sweet friend, a simple, yet extraordinary reminder:

You belong.

You belong.

You BELONG!

EXERCISE: Replace the names of Jacob and Israel with your own as you read the following verse out loud.

> *"But now, (O Jacob), listen to the Lord who created you. (O Israel),*
> *the one who formed you says, 'Do not be afraid, for I have*
> *ransomed you, I have called you by name; you are mine.'"*
> *—Isaiah 43:1, NLT*

EYES UP!

Don't look back! Eyes up and forward! Your best days are ahead of you, not behind. Don't get tangled up in shame, guilt, or regret. Remember, Christ has exchanged that old, decaying nature for His ever-regenerating life of truth, health, peace, and grace!

Superhero, you have much to accomplish! Much to give, so keep racing toward the finish line!

> *"I do have one compelling focus: I forget all of the past as I fasten my heart to the future instead. I run straight for the divine invitation of reaching the heavenly goal and gaining the victory-prize through the anointing of Jesus."*
> *—Philippians 3:13–14, TPT*

JOURNAL: What is in front of you? Discuss with the Lord and set a short-term goal for 3 months from today. Then a longer-range goal for one year. Describe them.

Thirty-Eight
FOCUS

Shame and regret are a trap built with snares of deception. They attempt to steal your gaze from the glorious vision in front of you. You must maintain your focus on Christ and the work He accomplished for you on the cross. He delivered you from all shame! He has opened a door to beautiful life!

> *"You've rescued me from hell and saved my life. You've crowned me*
> *with love and mercy. You satisfy my every desire with good things. You've*
> *supercharged my life so that I soar again like a flying eagle in the sky!*
> *You're a God who makes things right, giving justice to the defenseless."*
> *—Psalm 103:4–6, TPT*

JOURNAL: How has God crowned you with love and mercy?

What good things are in your future, even if they are in dream form right now?

Begin with the statement, "Thank you God for…"

Thirty-Nine
SET FREE

Make this declaration: "I am free! Nothing from the past has any power over me. I am hidden with God in Christ Jesus."

"Let me be clear, the Anointed One has set us free—not partially,
but completely and wonderfully free! We must always cherish this truth
and stubbornly refuse to go back into the bondage of our past."
—Galatians 5:1, TPT

JOURNAL: Write a prayer of gratitude for the freedom you have in Christ. "Thank you, God, for setting me free from…"

Forty

READY AT ALL TIMES

Jesus is the Word of God made flesh and bone! He is the breath of heaven, the Word spoken at creation: "Let there be light"—and there was light! He is the wisdom of ages, and you have His ear whenever, wherever—no restrictions!

Because you can have absolute confidence in this fact, you can be ready at all times. Ready with encouragement, support, and help for others. You are God's special envoy of peace!

What breathtaking truth!

"Love empowers us to fulfill the law of the Anointed One as we carry each other's troubles."
—Galatians 6:2, TPT

JOURNAL: How does the knowledge of the presence of Christ shift your current reality?

How does it empower you?

OPEN 24/7

The mind of Christ is available twenty-four hours a day, seven days a week. What do you need to know right now? Is there a challenge in front of you?

He has the answer! He has the ability! He is ready, willing, and able to provide exactly what you need—on time, in full, without fail!

"For who has known the Lord's mind, that he may instruct Him? But we have the mind of Christ."
—1 Corinthians 2:16, HCSB

JOURNAL: List the areas in which you need God's direct intervention and wisdom today.

Forty-Two
BLOOD & BREATH

Like blood in your veins and breath in your lungs, you require the Spirit and Word to live fully the life Christ has purposed. Human nature—the flesh—wants to draw you back to old ways of thinking and acting. The Word of God in union with the Holy Spirit, who is the living presence of Christ, supply all you need to overcome your flesh.

"I say then, walk by the Spirit and you will not carry out the desire of the flesh."
—Galatians 5:16, HCSB

JOURNAL: List three areas in which you have had victory through the Word and Spirit, and three areas in which you are still working toward victory.

VICTORY DANCE TODAY ~

VICTORY DANCE TOMORROW ~

Forty-Three
THE VOICE OF CALM

The Holy Spirit is present with you at all times. He is comfort in distress. He is power in weakness. He is knowledge when you don't have the answer.

Anxiety takes you places you don't need to go! The calming voice of your Father through the Holy Spirit steadies the helm, keeping you on course.

> *"But when He, the Spirit of truth, comes, He will guide you into all the truth; for He will not speak on His own initiative, but whatever He hears, He will speak; and He will disclose to you what is to come."*
> *—John 16:13, NASB*

JOURNAL: What struggles do you need Papa God to address right now? Are you in need of comfort? Knowledge? Power? Write it down and then *listen.*

Forty-Four

NEVER STOP LEARNING

It is vital to surround yourself with wise, experienced followers of Jesus Christ. You gain understanding and prudence as you listen carefully to their instruction and never stop learning.

> *"Stick close to my instruction, my son, and follow all my advice.*
> *If you do what I say you will live well. Guard your life with my*
> *revelation-truth, for my teaching is as precious as your eyesight."*
> *—Proverbs 7:1–2, TPT*

JOURNAL: Who are your wise counselors? Do you have favorite authors, online teachers, and bloggers?

A tribe is also important! These are trusted friends and mentors who *know* you and meet with you regularly—safe people to share your journey with. They pray with you and empower your growth. List them.

If you don't have a tribe yet, God is faithful! Ask Him; remember, He is in this with you and promises to supply every need you have (Philippians 4:19).

Forty-Five

GOOD FRIENDS OR IMPOSTERS

In this life there are good friends, and there are imposters. Good friends empower you to live the life God has called you to. They build up and amplify your voice. Imposters hold you back and silence your voice; silence and stalling out are not an option!

Embrace the good friends, hold them close and protect your relationship with them. Shed yourself of the imposters and don't look back. Mighty warrior, you have a high calling on your life, and you must pursue it!

"Because I love Zion, I will not keep still. Because my heart yearns for Jerusalem, I cannot remain silent. I will not stop praying for her until her righteousness shines like the dawn, and her salvation blazes like a burning torch."
—Isaiah 62:1, NLT

EXERCISE: Who is influencing you right now?

What are they speaking into your life?

How are they moving you in the direction of love?

Forty-Six
CALLED TO SERVE

You must be ever mindful of those you are here to serve. They are those within your realm of influence—a list that can change moment to moment. Think of the overwhelmed clerk at the check-out counter. The elderly man struggling with grocery sacks. Here's a good one: the cranky driver on the freeway. I know, that's a tough one! But the people you see and interact with every day are your ministry, your high trust from God!

"Don't let selfishness and prideful agendas take over. Embrace true humility, and lift your heads to extend love to others. Get beyond yourselves and protecting your own interests; be sincere, and secure your neighbors' interests first."
—Philippians 2:3–4, VOICE

EXERCISE: Name one person in your realm of influence you have the ability to serve.

Ask God to give you a word of life for that person. Be open to how He answers; it may be a special drawing, a little cash, some flowers, or a card. It may be as simple as a kind smile and a hand on the shoulder.

Write down what you plan to say or do, then return later and describe the experience.

Forty-Seven

WHAT GOD VALUES

God is love; kindness and respect are an inseparable aspect of His nature. God is honorable, always executing impartial justice. He places absolute importance on ethical conduct.

Your behavior is a direct reflection of your thought life—and your thought life is directly impacted by those who influence you. You are vitally influenced by those you spend time with. If you are to reflect the nature of God, you must be careful not to submit to negative influences!

> *"Whoever pursues justice and treats others with kindness*
> *discovers true life marked by integrity and respect."*
> *—Proverbs 21:21, VOICE*

JOURNAL: Describe the most influential relationships you currently have.

Forty-Eight
WEAR YOUR HELMET!

The head leads the heart, so nourish it with health! Protect it at all costs!

"Finally brothers and sisters, whatever is true, whatever is noble, whatever is right, whatever is pure, whatever is lovely, whatever is admirable— if anything is excellent or praiseworthy—think about such things."
—Philippians 4:8, NIV

JOURNAL: What steps are you currently taking to protect your thought life?

If you haven't been making a deliberate effort yet, take some time now to come up with a plan.

Forty-Nine

DRENCHED IN TRUTH

Truth is priceless. It is a substance of unquantifiable power. Truth liberates those who fully comprehend its meaning—it actually reshapes the mind! Christ desires to drench you in truth. Not just a little but overflowing and spilling all over the place!

"Immerse them in the truth, the truth Your voice speaks."
—John 17:17, VOICE

JOURNAL: List the truths you desire to fully comprehend! Are you seeking truth about your identity? The nature of God's love? How God sees you? GO!

LOVE IS A PERSON

Authentic love is more than deep emotional attachment—it is living and active. Love is embodied by Jesus Christ, our perfect example. Knowing Him is knowing love!

> *"Only God knows how much I dearly love you with the tender affection of Jesus, the Anointed One. I continue to pray for your love to grow and increase beyond measure, bringing you into the rich revelation of spiritual insight in all things."*
> *—Philippians 1:8–9, TPT*

JOURNAL: What are five distinct characteristics of Jesus Christ? It's okay, go deep on this! The Gospels of Matthew, Mark, Luke, and John are excellent resources.

Fifty-One
LOVE WITH SHOES ON

You are able to habitually walk out love by habitually soaking in the One who is love. Spend glorious hours mediating on Christ's Word, worshipping in His presence, being filled to the brim by His purity. Then, when you go out into the world—BAM! —you're love with shoes on!

"Those who are loved by God, let his love continually pour from you to one another, because God is love. Everyone who loves is fathered by God and experiences an intimate knowledge of him. The one who doesn't love has yet to know God, for God is love."
—1 John 4:7–8, TPT

JOURNAL: How have you personally experienced your Heavenly Father?

How does He speak to you? What is the tone of His voice? Does He have a favorite name for you? What is it?

Think of the details and jot as many down as you can.

MEDITATION

Even though it requires an eternity, go ahead, begin to revel in God's overwhelming love for you. Imagine how high, how wide and how deep His compassion goes. Envision the fathomless depths and rejoice!

"Then you will be empowered to discover what every holy one experiences—
the great magnitude of the astonishing love of Christ in all its dimensions. How deeply
intimate and far-reaching is his love! How enduring and inclusive it is! Endless love
beyond measurement that transcends our understanding—this extravagant love
pours into you until you are filled to overflowing with the fullness of God!"
—Ephesians 3:18–19, TPT

JOURNAL: What images come to your mind when attempting to visualize the measure of God's love? Gentle conversations of guidance? A private joke just between the two of you? Write down everything that comes to mind.

IT'S TIME TO FLY

Metamorphosis! The caterpillar sheds her skin, forming a hard, protective shell around her body. While sleeping inside, she dissolves into a wondrous concoction of goo. Within this goo is a miracle! Total transformation!

She emerges as a new creature with a whole new purpose! With beautiful wings, she looks and behaves nothing like a caterpillar. Instead of crawling from branch to branch, she glides on the wind! As she drinks nectar, her body pollinates the flowers, distributing life!

Like caterpillar to butterfly, we are being transformed, and soon it will be time to fly!

> *"So all of us who have had that veil removed can see and reflect the glory of the Lord. And the Lord—who is the Spirit—makes us more and more like him as we are changed into his glorious image."*
> *—2 Corinthians 3:18, NLT*

JOURNAL: We are being transformed into the same image as Jesus, who is the exact representation of God! Imagine what this means to you! Describe the changes taking place in the way you see yourself and your purpose.

Fifty-Four

A FAMILIAR FOG

Discouragement and self-doubt can settle in like a familiar fog. While it might be tempting to surrender, you must run to the face of God. He has new and wonderful things He is excited to share with you! When you quiet your heart and wait patiently, you will see God's blessings unfold before your eyes!

"If your faith remains strong, even while surrounded by life's difficulties, you will continue to experience the untold blessings of God! True happiness comes as you pass the test with faith and receive the victorious crown of life promised to every lover of God!"
—James 1:12, TPT

JOURNAL: Describe what happens when you experience discouragement and self-doubt. Are there any familiar habits or thoughts?

Now build a strategy to overcome. For example: Listening to worship music, quoting scripture out loud, or making truth declarations. List your ideas!

Fifty-Five

THE STAR MAKER

This new life you live blossoms through the work and word of Christ in you. In Him and through Him, you have all power and authority to fulfill your purpose.

Just think! The One who slung the entire solar system, all the stars you see and have yet to see, makes His home inside you! His voice, the voice of creation, echoes through you this very moment!

Self-doubt can be a mean tiger to tame but consider Jesus created the universe! Imagine what He is doing right now with you and me!

"My old identity has been co-crucified with Messiah and no longer lives;
for the nails of his cross crucified me with him. And now the essence of this new life
is no longer mine, for the Anointed One lives his life through me—we live in union
as one! My new life is empowered by the faith of the Son of God who loves me so
much that he gave himself for me and dispenses his life into mine!"
—Galatians 2:20, TPT

JOURNAL: How does this truth shift your thinking from self-doubt to Christ confidence?

Fifty-Six
ANCHOR THOUGHT

When we bellow in confusion, "God, I have NO idea what you're doing!" what are we truthfully asking? Brass tacks.

Our confusion is often cover for an underlying fear: "God, do You love me? Is any good going to come from this? Because right now, I don't see it."

When I'm going through these times, I need an anchor thought. An anchor thought is undeniable truth. What do I know about God's unchangeable nature?

"'My thoughts are nothing like your thoughts,' says the Lord. 'And my ways are far beyond anything you could imagine. For just as the heavens are higher than the earth, so my ways are higher than your ways and my thoughts higher than your thoughts.'"
—Isaiah 55:8–9, NLT

JOURNAL: My anchor thought is "God is *love*. Everything He is and does is born in *love*." What is yours?

PERFECT POWER

God's perfect power never stops. As you move deeper in union with Christ, your perspective expands and sharpens! In the words of the scripture below, you receive the "full revelation of God"!

That is amazing! Mind-boggling, in fact! This understanding is meant to fill you with abundant confidence! You are fully equipped to carry out God's purpose for your life!

"For you have acquired new creation life which is continually being renewed into the likeness of the One who created you; giving you the full revelation of God."
—Colossians 3:10, TPT

JOURNAL: The full revelation of God! What thoughts does this biblical promise inspire within you?

How has God expanded your perspective so far?

Describe the impact this gift has on your vision for the future.

Fifty-Eight

THE SHARK DENTIST

Cristina Zenato has devoted her life to sharks. She's known as the shark dentist, pulling fish hooks from the mouths of toothy, terrifying creatures!

The sharks come from all over the ocean and patiently allow her to perform this kindness! Sometimes the hooks are lodged in delicate places, and only after multiple visits is Cristina able to pull them free. When she's done, they nuzzle her in gratitude, showering her with sharky affection! Truly a miracle of God's compassion!

We each have a job in caring not just for other people but also the world God made. That job is revealed in our passions! For Cristina, it's shark dentistry! For you and me, maybe not, but think carefully—what do you love? Furry animals, reptiles, forests, gardens?

What you love is what you're responsible for.

> *"We have a special role in His plan. He calls us to life by His message*
> *of truth so that we will show the rest of His creatures His goodness and love."*
> *—James 1:18, VOICE*

JOURNAL: What part of creation is most precious to you?

How might you take a lifelong responsibility for it?

Fifty-Nine

SOMETHING EXTRAORDINARY

When you came into a covenant with Jesus Christ, you agreed to devote your body to God as His holy temple. The life you live is a tributary of all He is: His essence, power, wisdom, nature, and word, now flowing through you!

You are something extraordinary. You are a living sanctuary where people experience the Kingdom of God.

"By living in God, love has been brought to its full expression in us so that we may fearlessly face the day of judgment, because all that Jesus now is, so are we in this world."
—1 John 4:17, TPT

JOURNAL: What a powerful truth: *"All that Jesus now is, so are we in this world"*! How does this shape your understanding of who you are?

Sixty

ABIDE

The possibilities are unlimited! You make your spiritual home in Jesus Christ, and He makes His home within you! You abide in Him.

The word "abide" means to dwell, live, become one, and be held continually. Think about it! You are in Christ Jesus, the Creator, and He is in you!

> *"But if you live in life-union with me and if my words live powerfully within you—then you can ask whatever you desire, and it will be done."*
> *—John 15:7, TPT*

JOURNAL: Wow! Look at the authority Jesus bestows upon you! How does this truth form your identity? What does it do for your confidence?

Sixty-One
WHAT WE BELIEVE

When you truly believe a fact or idea, your behavior proves your conviction. Your belief system is manifested in your decisions, your words, and your actions. What do you believe?

"So above all, guard the affections of your heart, for they affect all that you are. Pay attention to the welfare of your innermost being, for from there flows the wellspring of life."
—Proverbs 4:23, TPT

JOURNAL: Name one thing you truly believe.

How has this belief shaped your behavior and life choices?

Sixty-Two

THE MOUTH REVEALS THE HEART

By attentive listening, you'll know instantly what is occupying your mind and shaping your decisions. What fills our thoughts is revealed by the words flowing from our mouth. Pay careful attention to them. The mouth reveals the heart!

"For whatever is in your heart determines what you say. A good person produces good things from the treasury of a good heart, and an evil person produces evil things from the treasury of an evil heart."
—Matthew 12:34–35, NLT

JOURNAL: Think a moment about the words you hear coming from your mouth on a consistent basis. Write them down so you can see them with your eyes.

What do they reveal?

Sixty-Three

THE BEST SOAP EVER!

Key ingredients in renewing the mind: a shift in belief, the filling of the Holy Spirit, and the regenerating power of God's Word. These gifts from God are like the best soap ever and have a miraculous effect when applied! The sinful actions in our past are swept away in the river of God's super-abundant grace, replaced by the life of Jesus Christ!

> *"But when the kindness of God our Savior and His love for mankind appeared, He saved us—not by works of righteousness that we had done, but according to His mercy, through the washing of regeneration and renewal by the Holy Spirit."*
> *—Titus 3:4–5, HCSB*

JOURNAL: God's grace has made you into a completely different human! How does this knowledge shift your perspective?

How does it combat toxic shame and condemnation?

Sixty-Four

EXPECT GOOD THINGS

Knowledge of the Lord creates peace, safety, and beauty. Draw near to Him with an expectation of good. He loves and enjoys you!

> *"None will harm or destroy another on My entire holy mountain, for the land will be as full of the knowledge of the Lord as the sea is filled with water."*
> —**Isaiah 11:9, HCSB**

EXERCISE: Run an Internet search for *"What does the Bible say about the nature of God?"* Write a selection on stickies and place them on your mirror.

Meditate on them for one full week. Share the results! Go to *toxictotransformedlife.com*.

Sixty-Five

BEYOND SPACE & TIME

God lives outside of time. God lives beyond the confines of space. God is love, boundless and unstoppable. When He loves, it is with the scope and measure of eternity. God loves you!

> ***"Long ago the Lord said to Israel: 'I have loved you, my people, with an everlasting love. With unfailing love I have drawn you to myself.'"***
> ***—Jeremiah 31:3, NLT***

EXERCISE: Read today's Bible passage out loud using your name.

"Long ago the Lord said to me, 'I have loved you, _____, with an everlasting love. With unfailing love I have drawn you to myself.'"

Sixty-Six
INFLUENCE

Jesus is full of grace and truth. He always guides the listener to empowerment without condemnation and shame. You grow stronger as you surround yourself with teachers reflecting the heart and mind of Jesus. He is not concerned with outward, superficial matters! He is concerned with a healthy heart and mind. He loves you, the individual, right to the core!

> *"Stop judging based on the superficial. First you must embrace the standards of mercy and truth."*
> *—John 7:24, TPT*

JOURNAL: Think about your primary influencers right now. What do you hear when they speak?

How do they influence you?

Sixty-Seven

TRUST YOUR GUT!

One troubling injury of verbal and emotional abuse is a deadening of discernment. In casual terms, you lose the ability to trust your gut. You may feel something's off, but then ignore it because you've been told so many times what you feel doesn't matter. This kills your ability to be prudent, to see trouble ahead and avoid it! But the Holy Spirit will empower you to recognize truth once more. He will bring your gut back to life!

"Dear friends, do not believe everyone who claims
to speak by the Spirit. You must test them to see if the spirit they have
comes from God. For there are many false prophets in the world."
—1 John 4:1, NLT

JOURNAL: List 5 benefits of trusting your gut! Begin each statement with *"Through Christ I_____."*
Example: *Through Christ I have the ability to spot trouble ahead and avoid it.*

Sixty-Eight
LIFE & FREEDOM

The voice of God is the voice of life, freedom, joy, and truth. The voice of shame is a thief and a liar. Its only purpose is to enslave, kill, and destroy. Be mindful of which voice you give attention to.

> *"A thief has only one thing in mind—he wants to steal,*
> *slaughter, and destroy. But I have come to give you everything in*
> *abundance, more than you expect—life in its fullness until you overflow!"*
> *—John 10:10, TPT*

JOURNAL: Shame always has a target, and its purpose is control. Where does shame target you most?

Now give careful attention to the Holy Spirit and ask for His words of life to replace the voice of shame.

Write down what you hear and declare that freedom out loud. He may lead you to a particular passage in the Bible; write it down! He may say something very short.

All this is good! It's from Him! It is important to learn to *hear* God's voice and trust that it is Him speaking!

Sixty-Nine

A DIVINE WORK OF ART

Just look at you! You're positively amazing! A divine work of art! Living poetry of the Most High God! Wow! Just stand back and take a moment to appreciate the gorgeous work of Creator God.

His fingers must have moved with such delicate precision when He made you! Can you imagine the tickled smile on His face as He put the finishing touches on your little nose and ears?

Think about all the dreams He has for you! All the adventures you are about to experience with Him! It's astounding! You know, you are important to Him.

Yes, you are a priceless asset in the Kingdom purposes of God!

> *"I thank you, God, for making me so mysteriously complex!*
> *Everything you do is marvelously breathtaking. It simply amazes*
> *me to think about it! How thoroughly you know me, Lord!"*
> *—Psalm 139:14, TPT*

JOURNAL: Verbal and emotional abuse do extreme damage to your ability to see as God sees. Beloved, when God looks at you, He sees His most favorite work of art! He sees an absolute masterpiece!

It is vital for you to see through the eyes of your Creator and be in awe of what He has done!

Write down five amazing qualities God has created within you, including physical, intellectual, and emotional attributes. Begin each statement, *"Thank you God for creating me with_____."*

Seventy

YOUR LIFE MATTERS!

Your life matters. You were intentionally created with a specific assignment in mind—an assignment only you can accomplish. Yes, precious child of God, you have purpose and a reason to live!

"We have become his poetry, a re-created people that will fulfill the destiny he has given each of us, for we are joined to Jesus, the Anointed One. Even before we were born, God planned in advance our destiny and the good works we would do to fulfill it!"
—Ephesians 2:10, TPT

JOURNAL: What are you passionate about? When you imagine that one thing you could do non-stop for the rest of your life, what is it? These are the ingredients of your destiny!

Seventy-One
DESTINY WITHIN YOU

God's eyes rove the corners of the earth looking for people the rest of the world overlooks. Joseph and David were bullied by their family members. Ruth was a poor widow with no social status. Peter, James, and John were simple fishermen with no credentials. Matthew was a tax man. Yet each one carried a powerful destiny!

Your credentials don't matter! What matters is your willingness to do whatever the Heavenly Father asks. When you give Him that, He'll turn the world upside-down!

"Brothers and sisters, consider who you were when God called you to salvation. Not many of you were wise scholars by human standards, nor were many of you in positions of power. Not many of you were considered the elite when you answered God's call. But God chose those whom the world considers foolish to shame those who think they are wise, and God chose the puny and powerless to shame the high and mighty. He chose the lowly, the laughable in the world's eyes— nobodies—so that he would shame the somebodies. For he chose what is regarded as insignificant in order to supersede what is regarded as prominent."
—1 Corinthians 1:26–28, TPT

JOURNAL: Ask the Holy Spirit right now, "What was I created for?"

Write down everything He brings to mind. Remember, His voice will always be a voice of kindness, hope, and empowerment!

Seventy-Two

GOD LOVES YOU

Your value lies in who you are: a child of God, His offspring, a co-heir with Christ! Being diligent is important, but understand, your value and worth in the eyes of God have nothing to do with performance!

You cannot earn God's love; you cannot work hard enough or skillfully enough to obtain it. Why? You already have it in abundance!

"Throughout the coming ages we will be the visible display of the infinite, limitless riches of his grace and kindness, which was showered upon us in Jesus Christ."
—Ephesians 2:7, TPT, emphasis added

JOURNAL: Describe the difference between walking through life in the knowledge that you *are* accepted versus trying to *earn* acceptance.

Seventy-Three
ALL YOU NEED TO KNOW

Jesus Christ crucified and risen from the dead. According to the apostle Paul, if this is all you know, you are highly equipped for powerful, effective Kingdom work. Paul was trained by the best scholars of his day and was considered an elite in his field. Yet, when it came to his Kingdom assignment, he left all that behind.

> *"For I determined to know nothing among you except Jesus Christ, and Him crucified."*
> *—1 Corinthians 2:2, NASB*

JOURNAL: How have you limited yourself with false expectations—phrases like *"I don't know enough"*?

If your knowledge of Jesus and the power of the Holy Spirit are enough, how does that set you free?

Seventy-Four

THE SEED

Within you is a seed! It is planted deep in your spirit: The Word of God. The same Word spoken at creation! The same Word that raised Jesus from the dead!

That power lives in you as a seed! Nurture the seed by worshiping God, by praying and listening to Him, by soaking in the Bible!

Remember the caterpillar: A metamorphosis takes place and the dead places come alive! The barren ground bursts with new life, filling the landscape with abundance!

> *"For through the eternal and living Word of God*
> *you have been born again. And this 'seed' that he planted within you*
> *can never be destroyed but will live and grow inside of you forever."*
> *—1 Peter 1:23, TPT*

JOURNAL: List your strategies for nurturing the seed of God's Word in your life.

Seventy-Five

RENOVATION UNDERWAY

Renovation makes the old new again! A skilled craftsman demolishes a crooked, unstable wall, replacing it with new construction that will endure.

This is exactly what is happening with your mind—renovation! But it takes time and patient endurance. It takes steady building and the careful selection of materials.

By faithfully applying God's Word to your mind, you tear out the rotten and replace it with the living!

"His divine power has granted to us everything pertaining to life and godliness, through the true knowledge of Him who called us by His own glory and excellence. For by these He has granted to us His precious and magnificent promises, so that by them you may become partakers of the divine nature, having escaped the corruption that is in the world by lust."
—2 Peter 1:3–4, NASB

JOURNAL: What progress have you experienced so far in your renovation?

Seventy-Six

THE LAND OF LIMITLESS

In Christ you live in the land of limitless! You have access to limitless grace, limitless peace, limitless expectation of good! Each sunrise ushers in the new!

New mercy washes away your shame. You receive new strength for endurance to carry on. Everything you need is yours with the breaking of each new dawn!

"And the one sitting on the throne said, 'Look, I am making everything new!'
And then he said to me, 'Write this down, for what I tell you is trustworthy and true.'"
—Revelation 21:5, NLT

JOURNAL: How is Christ is making all things new in your thoughts and emotions?

Seventy-Seven
TRUTH & LIFE

Words of life transform, renew, and give! They give healing, strength, and refreshment. They give real solutions, courage, and hope! They energize, restore, and cleanse. We are always better for having listened to words of life!

"A reliable, trustworthy messenger refreshes the heart…
like a gentle breeze blowing at harvest time."
—Proverbs 25:13, TPT

JOURNAL: Write a word of life and share it with me at *toxictotransformedlife.com*. It does not have to be long or loaded with fancy poetry; it simply needs to be true, kind, and encouraging!

Seventy-Eight

AUTHENTIC LOVE

Bank tellers are trained to recognize a counterfeit by learning what authentic currency looks, feels, and smells like. Why don't they study up on counterfeits instead? Because counterfeits have innumerable variations and constantly change. It would be impossible to learn them all. But authentic currency is always the same and rarely changes. By becoming an expert on real currency, they recognize a fake immediately!

The truth always exposes the false regardless of how cleverly it is disguised!

To help us avoid counterfeit substitutes for love, 1 Corinthians 13 shows us what authentic love looks and behaves like. Once you know love's nature and become intimately acquainted with all of its ways, this knowledge will serve as a guardian of your heart and mind!

"Love is patient and kind. Love is not jealous or boastful or proud or rude. It does not demand its own way. It is not irritable, and it keeps no record of being wronged. It does not rejoice about injustice but rejoices whenever the truth wins out. Love never gives up, never loses faith, is always hopeful, and endures through every circumstance."
—1 Corinthians 13:4–7, NLT

JOURNAL: First Corinthians 13 provides us with a litmus test of love. Describe how you will use it to recognize love in yourself and others.

Seventy-Nine

THIS IS OUR GOD!

Jesus the Anointed leads you into all knowledge. He breaks the power of deception. He heals and restores. He embraces with tender affection. He will never abandon you! He is pure, unadulterated love! He made you by hand and accepts you with sheer delight!

Jesus filled with grace and truth—this is our God!

"For the Law was given through Moses; grace
and truth were realized through Jesus Christ."
—John 1:17, NASB

JOURNAL: Let's unpack the verse above. *Grace* is favor, acceptance, kindness, and love. *Truth* is the reality of a matter—what it genuinely is. To *realize* in this context is to make complete or bring something into being.

What do grace and truth mean to you?

LIFE TO THE FULL!

Christ's vision is for you to have "life to the full"! This is a life of health and prosperity surrounded by people who are filled with kindness, generosity, and wisdom.

> *"The thief comes only in order to steal and kill and destroy. I came that they may have and enjoy life, and have it in abundance (to the full, till it overflows)."*
> *—John 10:10, AMP*

JOURNAL: Take an inventory of the people, places, and things you currently associate with.

How do they motivate you?

How do they empower you?

Eighty-One
BEAUTIFUL BOUNDARIES

Boundaries are beautiful! Boundaries define parameters of healthy, loving interaction. God uses boundaries! He defines what is pleasing and displeasing to Him. He communicates these boundaries clearly in His Word and supplies the Holy Spirit to make sure you understand and follow His instruction.

You are free to define what a healthy, prosperous relationship with you should look like. As a unique individual, you have your own tastes and preferences. It is perfectly acceptable to determine and communicate those tastes and preferences. For example, if you hate scary movies, it's valid to communicate it as a boundary: "I do not like scary movies; instead, let's watch something we both enjoy."

Boundaries protect health and vitality within relationships!

"And this I pray, that your love may abound still more and more in real knowledge and all discernment, so that you may approve the things that are excellent, in order to be sincere and blameless until the day of Christ."
—Philippians 1:9–10, NASB

JOURNAL: Describe a healthy boundary for you. What does it look like?

How will it protect you and your relationships?

Eighty-Two
PACE YOURSELF!

It's a marathon, not a sprint. Pace yourself! Keep going; the victory is at the finish line! God's got you, so you've got this!

"And let endurance have its perfect result, so that you
may be perfect and complete, lacking in nothing."
—James 1:4, NASB

"Those who are victorious will sit with me on my throne,
just as I was victorious and sat with my Father on his throne."
—Revelation 3:21, NLT

JOURNAL: Move at a pace you can sustain for the long haul. Ask yourself the following:

Am I getting enough rest?

Am I eating healthily?

Am I working at a sustainable pace?

Where can I grow?

Eighty-Three

THE POWER OF REST

A key ingredient in healing is physical rest! In order to regenerate the mind, you need regular intervals of tranquility and refreshment. Good sleep, walks, fresh air, and sunshine are vital to health. So is laughter and fun! This is all part of rest. You must take time each week and invest in your own healing!

"There was such a swirl of activity around Jesus, with so many people coming and going, that they were unable to even eat a meal. So Jesus said to his disciples, 'Come, let's take a break and find a secluded place where you can rest a while.'"
—*Mark 6:31, TPT*

"He offers a resting place for me in his luxurious love.
His tracks take me to an oasis of peace, the quiet brook of bliss."
—*Psalm 23:2, TPT*

JOURNAL: A simple way to view rest is the term "self-care." This is not the same as selfishness!

Self-care revitalizes the spirit, soul, mind, and body so they can perform at the highest possible levels of love! Jesus practiced "self-care" regularly! How will you?

Eighty-Four
TROLLS

Fear is nothing but a nasty little troll, his tiny fists banging the air as he screeches, "You're going to fail!"

Jesus is truth and love. He stands glorious with resurrection light, saying, "You cannot fail, because I AM with you!"

> *"Love never brings fear, for fear is always related to punishment. But love's perfection drives the fear of punishment far from our hearts. Whoever walks constantly afraid of punishment has not reached love's perfection."*
> *—1 John 4:18, TPT*

JOURNAL: Do you have a troll problem? Describe it.

How does love free you from the fear of punishment? Punishment manifests in many forms: shame, guilt, embarrassment, etc.

How will you move forward?

FALSE ALARM

Have you learned to live with a false alarm shattering the tranquility of your mind? This sense of impending failure, shame, or embarrassment is known as anxiety.

It's time to remove the alarm, pull out the batteries, and toss it in the trash can! Christ, who is your life, provides all you need by filling you with the Holy Spirit.

You have discernment, truth, adequacy, power, love, and soundness of mind. In Christ you have everything you need for life, and life to the full!

"When Christ, who is our life, is revealed,
then you also will be revealed with Him in glory."
—Colossians 3:4, NASB

"Let your heart be always guided by the peace of the Anointed One,
who called you to peace as part of his one body. And always be thankful.
Let the word of Christ live in you richly, flooding you with all wisdom."
—Colossians 3:15–16, TPT

JOURNAL: The Holy Spirit frees you from the clutches of anxiety with truth and real solutions. How will you trust Him and let Him work in your life?

Eighty-Six

THE WAY OF LOVE

Genesis 1 describes the moment of creation. God hovered over the surface of the earth and saw it was "formless and void," and then He began methodically bringing order and form to that mass of nothing. Soon He had something spectacular! A lush garden, furry animals, slithery reptiles, birds, and fish!

He is doing the same thing in your mind right now! He is speaking peace, understanding, and clear direction. He is building something awesome within you, beloved! He is teaching you the way of love!

"In the beginning God created the heavens and the earth. The earth was formless and void, and darkness was over the surface of the deep, and the Spirit of God was moving over the surface of the waters. Then God said, 'Let there be light'; and there was light."
—Genesis 1:1–3, NASB

JOURNAL: How are you experiencing God's creative power within your mind?

How is it impacting you day by day?

Eighty-Seven
ESCAPE THE GROUND LOOP!

In awful moments, sometimes out of nowhere, it all starts crashing in! Wave upon wave, tormenting thoughts and memories catapult you into anxious turmoil. Like a plane rotating wildly in a ground loop, escape feels hopeless! You may be tempted to give in, but with small, intentional steps toward light, you have a way of escape!

First, you must breathe! Deep, slow, steady breaths! The oxygen slows down your pulse and creates calm. Then, physically grab a solid surface, a table, or even the floor; physically pull yourself back into the here and now, escaping your bad memories.

Once you do these things, you can sit down and inhale the truth of God's Word. Allow His Holy Spirit to minister comfort and peace to your mind and soul. Rescue is here!

> *"I ponder all you've done, Lord, musing on all your miracles….*
> *By your glory-bursts you've rescued us over and over."*
> *—Psalm 77:12, 15, TPT*

EXERCISE: Anxiety attacks often happen as you recover from verbal and emotional abuse. Being aware and prepared places power back in your hands.

Create your "ground loop" escape plan!

Eighty-Eight

ROCKY!

In the award-winning movie, "Rocky" our under-dog hero, Rocky Balboa defeats heavy weight champion, Apollo Creed, by refusing to stay down. Just like Rocky Balboa, it's not about how many times you fall, it's about how many times you get up!

You are only defeated when you fail to get up. God is for you! He is the lifter of your head. You have immeasurable strength because when you are weak, He is strong.

Keep getting up!

"For the lovers of God may suffer adversity and stumble
seven times, but they will continue to rise over and over again."
—Proverbs 24:16, TPT

JOURNAL: Time for a victory dance! Write your Rocky Balboa story: How have you overcome by refusing to stay down? I'd love to hear about it. Will you share at *toxictotransformedlife.com*?

Eighty-Nine

UNSEEN POWER

Endurance for believers in Jesus Christ is not an earthly, natural power but supernatural. You cannot see it with human eyes. It lies within your spirit, un-confined by the limits of physical strength. For you, endurance flows from faith in the Holy Spirit through whom all things are possible! You have unseen power in unlimited supply!

"So no wonder we don't give up. For even though our outer person gradually wears out, our inner being is renewed every single day…. We don't focus our attention on what is seen but on what is unseen. For what is seen is temporary, but the unseen realm is eternal."
—2 Corinthians 4:16, 18, TPT

JOURNAL: The strength that comes from God never becomes fatigued! It never fails! Describe what this truth means to you and your journey of transforming the mind.

THE POWER OF PATIENCE

Patience strengthens resolve, and resolve is what empowers endurance. Patience is the substance of self-control, a virtue that the Holy Spirit imparts to you through faith! Whatever you face, have faith that God has it all under His sovereign power and oversight. Have confidence that He is getting the situation handled and all you need do is wait! He will give you direction and a perfect solution. God is just, and He will never let you down!

"Teach the older men to exercise self-control, to be worthy of respect, and to live wisely. They must have sound faith and be filled with love and patience."
—Titus 2:2, NLT

JOURNAL: Think of a situation you've been facing. How does shifting your focus to confidence in God empower your resolve?

Ninety-One
DILIGENCE

Healing the mind requires diligence—constant, persistent effort. You cannot afford to be careless or quit halfway through the process. No, dear friend, press through and reap the reward!

Imagine standing in front of the mirror, a wise, courageous, compassionate face smiling back at you! That is what lies just ahead, and it's only the beginning! God has so many good things in store! Keep at it! You are doing marvelously!

"Watch over your heart with all diligence, for from it flow the springs of life."
—Proverbs 4:23, NASB

JOURNAL: How have you applied diligence in the past?

How did it make you feel?

How will you continue to apply diligence as you work to transform your mind?

Ninety-Two
THE BATTLE

The battle for emotional healing is waged first in the mind, which compels the heart to follow. This battle is for your thought life and what controls it. This is a spiritual battle, and therefore the weapons are also spiritual. Careful application of God's Word empowered by the Holy Spirit will guarantee your triumph! Then you will be fully equipped to lead others to victory!

"Now we have received, not the spirit of the world, but the Spirit who is from God, so that we may know the things freely given to us by God, which things we also speak, not in words taught by human wisdom, but in those taught by the Spirit, combining spiritual thoughts with spiritual words."
—1 Corinthians 2:12–13, NASB

JOURNAL: How is the battle for your mind a spiritual battle?

How have you seen this to be true personally?

Prayerfully consider the question: What is my spiritual battle plan?

Ninety-Three
LIFELINE

Prayer is your lifeline! God has made a way to stay in continual, never-ceasing communion with Him through this precious, life-sustaining expression. You are free to talk to God in the car, the gym, and the grocery store. Prayer can be as natural as breathing!

"Don't be pulled in different directions or worried about a thing. Be saturated in prayer throughout each day, offering your faith-filled requests before God with overflowing gratitude. Tell him every detail of your life, then God's wonderful peace that transcends human understanding will make the answers known to you through Jesus Christ."
—Philippians 4:6–7 TPT

JOURNAL: How do you view prayer?

Where do you spend time in prayer? Do you make use of a favorite comfy chair? Do you pray on your morning commute?

Do you like to journal your prayers? (That's one of my favorite ways!)

Ninety-Four

NO SMALL THING!

Being a child of God is no small thing. You have tremendous privilege and power in your royal family position. You carry the Spirit of Almighty God; you carry the glory of God in your body! You can ask anything from your Father, knowing He hears and grants your request! You have access to all He knows, sees, and hears because you have the mind of Christ. You carry His Kingdom authority and presence everywhere you go! No, this is no small thing!

"For God knew his people in advance, and he chose them to become like his Son, so that his Son would be the firstborn among many brothers and sisters."
—Romans 8:29, NLT

JOURNAL: How does the truth about your royal status impact your thinking?

How does it impact your self-worth?

How does it impact your confidence?

Ninety-Five
STRENGTH IN NUMBERS

There is never a good time to be a loner, but especially not when you are in a time of healing. War is won by the strength of numbers! God never intended for us to be alone; in fact, it is the one thing He singled out at creation as NOT good (Genesis 2:18).

> *"It takes a grinding wheel to sharpen a blade,*
> *and so one person sharpens the character of another."*
> *—Proverbs 27:17, TPT*

JOURNAL: Who is sharpening your character?

How do you sharpen each other?

What fruit is being produced as a result of your friendship?

Ninety-Six

LOVE & WISDOM

The Lord is faithful! The Lord is kind! All He does is founded in His absolute nature of love and wisdom. He has perfect intentions for your life! He earnestly desires good for your destiny. He has a path for you that leads to abundant success and wellbeing. You can trust Him!

"Your kingdom is an everlasting kingdom; Your rule is for all generations. The Lord is faithful in all His words and gracious in all His actions."
—Psalm 145:13, HCSB

JOURNAL: How do you imagine your future?

What do you hope to be doing in six months and one year?

PRINCE OF PEACE

Christ Jesus is the Prince of Peace. You experience His peace as you allow His presence the right to govern your heart and mind.

"And let the peace that comes from Christ rule in your hearts. For as members of one body you are called to live in peace. And always be thankful."
—Colossians 3:15, NLT

JOURNAL: What does it mean to you to let the peace of Christ rule your heart? How does it look? What are the results?

What are some practical routines that can facilitate your submission to the peace of Christ?

Ninety-Eight

CONFOUNDED AWE

Stand before the Lord of all creation in confounded awe! Take a moment and soak in the majesty of all He is. Open your mind; comprehend how vast His knowledge, how expansive His awareness, how timeless His wisdom. Always try to begin the day from this perspective.

"The [reverent] fear of the Lord [that is, worshiping Him and regarding Him as truly awesome] is the beginning and the preeminent part of knowledge [its starting point and its essence]. But arrogant fools despise [skillful and godly] wisdom and instruction and self-discipline."
—Proverbs 1:7, AMP

JOURNAL: Just try to imagine God. Take 30 seconds and meditate on who He is.

What images came to mind?

What is your understanding of who God is?

Ninety-Nine

LIVE THE TRUTH

It is time to live the truth of who you are! In Christ, you are a new creation. You are His body, His bride, His priest. You are powerful, filled with resurrection life.

You are intelligent, holding within you the mind of Creator God! You change the atmosphere; every room you walk into gushes with Kingdom light!

You are a child of God and coheir with Christ! You have everything you ask in Jesus' name!

"For it is not from man that we draw our life but from God
as we are being joined to Jesus, the Anointed One. And now he is our
God-given wisdom, our virtue, our holiness, and our redemption."
—1 Corinthians 1:30, TPT

JOURNAL: Using *"I am"* statements, write down who you are.

One Hundred

THE VALLEY OF DRY BONES

The ancient prophet Ezekiel received a vision from the Lord. In it, he was taken to a valley filled with human bones. They were dry, having baked for years in the hot desert sun. As they stood there together looking over the ancient battlefield, the Lord asked Ezekiel an astonishing question: "Can these bones live?"

I imagine the prophet being wholly at sea: "Is this a trick question? These people are dead. Not just a little dead—a lot dead, nothing-to-work-with dead. No lungs, no heart, nothing!"

Ezekiel, not dissuaded, came up with a pretty decent answer: "Lord, you know!" God then directed him to do something incomprehensible: "Prophesy life to the bones!"

Ezekiel was a faithful friend and servant to God. It never mattered how outrageous the request; he always followed through. This particular day was no different. He prophesied to the bones.

Next, the most beautiful, amazing thing he had ever witnessed: The bones began to regenerate! New muscles, ligaments, and skin clothed those dusty, ancient bones! Finally, they stood up, fully alive with breath in their lungs, and became a living, powerful army!

Beloved warrior, the Almighty is standing beside you, just as He did with Ezekiel. What do you see? Dreams baked dry in the desert sun. Desires of the heart left forgotten in the sand.

Dreams are but visions of purpose yet to be fulfilled. You may feel they are long past any hope of life, yet God, your beloved Heavenly Papa, is asking, "Can these bones live?"

"'Speak a prophetic message to these bones and say, "Dry bones,
listen to the word of the Lord! This is what the Sovereign Lord says:
Look I am going to put breath into you and make you live again!"'"
—Ezekiel 37:4–5, NLT

EXERCISE: What dreams do you see lying on the battlefield? Can these bones live?

A PERSONAL REQUEST

AMAZON REVIEW: I want to let you know how much I appreciate you! I pray this devotional facilitates deeper levels of growth and freedom in your life! If it does, I would like to make a request of support.

Would you please write a short review on the Amazon page? Your reviews are life to authors! We literally cannot survive without them!

TOUCH OTHERS WITH FREEDOM: Beyond surviving as an author, there is another, even more important reason to write a review. It is extremely helpful to others! That is particularly true for this book!

When you provide a review, you will help to guide others on a journey of transformation! You will encourage them to continue! Your simple review could be the difference between someone pursuing healing and staying stuck. You will touch others with freedom!

DROP ME A LINE: Please drop me a line on my website as well, located at _toxictotransformedlife.com_. I eagerly anticipate reading your journey of transformation.

MY GRATITUDE: I wish I could fully communicate how grateful I am for you! How deeply I honor your courage! How much I pray for all things beautiful in your present and future! Thank you, thank you, thank you for being part of my life!

Donna L Lewis

MY HEARTFELT THANKS

My husband, Jade Lewis. Your kindness, patience, and healing love have been the arms of God around my life! You have filled me with constant words of life since the day we met! You are my inspiration, my world, and I love you forever, "truly, madly, deeply"!

To my family—Betty, Jim, Deni, Rick, Shelly, Dave, Jon, and Ellen and all the rest of you! Each family gathering is an expression of sincere love, devotion, and kindness. You breathe life into everyone you touch. I love you so much; how blessed I am to call you family!

To my children, Ariel, Tiffanie, and William. You keep me going and I love you with all my heart!

To Jennifer Hayes Yates, my accountability partner and friend. You are a gift from God! Your wisdom, encouragement, and experience has been invaluable to me through this process. I thank you and bless you abundantly!

To Gary Williams, my SPS Coach, thank you so much. Your constant encouragement and wise counsel have been priceless. I cannot imagine doing this without you.

Chandler Bolt, Self-Publishing School and the Mastermind Community, THANK YOU! I am grateful, so grateful for the resources, support, and education you provide. You have facilitated and empowered the dreams of so many, today I am one of them. May you be blessed abundantly and continue for years and years to come.

To Paul Wonders on Reedsy, my editor. You have done a remarkable job. Thank you for your hard work and talent in clarifying the message while staying true to my voice.

To Jen Henderson of Wild Words Formatting. I am ever grateful for the beautiful presentation of this book. Outstanding!

Angie, pro_ebookcovers on Fiverr. Thank you for the fabulous work on the book cover design. You are amazing!

With all my heart,
Donna L Lewis

DONNA L LEWIS, AUTHOR

I sat, a green as grass 18-year-old, in my very first college class. Dr. Olds, perched on the platform a few feet away. He was a slight built man wearing a tidy suit and tie. His horn-rimmed glasses glinted in the high auditorium lights. "He looks friendly enough" I mused hopefully.

Then he described our primary assignment, "I expect each one of you to keep a regular journal. You will turn it in every Friday." My heart froze. My eyes narrowed. "He shall be known as Horn Rims, killer of dreams!"

Spelling and organizing words presented a gargantuan task, one that terrified me. Throughout high school anything that had to be hand written was my stone of stumbling and rock of offense. I could never get past first draft. My demise always came inscribed with bright red ink, "F".

For a moment I lost myself, imagining the professor morphing into Darth Vader. He stood ominously, red Bic Pen light saber humming and glowing at his side. Eying me through his horn-rims with vile glee, he raises the Bic saber. I clutch the pitiful composition book to my chest, ready for vaporization. Then, suddenly, a crisp, yet strangely warm voice brought me back to the auditorium.

It was Horn Rims, "Don't worry about spelling or grammar". You could have knocked me over with an Ewok. "Is he serious?" I leaned in completely intrigued.

"The point is to write, just get the words out. You cannot do that if you're worried about spelling and grammar!" I saw hearts and stars as Horn Rims morphed back to Dr. Olds.

"Dr. Olds," my heart bloomed, "the Obi Wan to my Skywalker. I love this man!"

Dr. Olds, with his assignment, opened a world to me I never believed could exist. The world of words and expressing my heart through them. That was 1984. I have kept a journal every day since then.

I don't have Dr. Olds anymore, but I do have the best Obi Wan a girl could ask for, my awesome God. I share all my ideas, thoughts and dreams with Him. I listen as He speaks to me through the Holy Spirit and record every word.

One such dream you hold in your hands today. The dream of becoming an author.

Thank you Dr. Olds, thank you sweet and precious reader.

Thank you, Papa-God…

CPSIA information can be obtained
at www.ICGtesting.com
Printed in the USA
LVHW061454291021
701926LV00014B/473

9 780578 530994